Are you ready for an Art Attack?

Creating collages is brilliant fun! 'Collage' means sticking down bits of paper, card and other things to make pictures. You can get some terrific effects. You can build up layers, create 3D pictures and make collages that sparkle and shine!

So if you're ready to go collage crazy turn the page and let's have some Art Attacks!

CONTENTS

D1321606

...ler: Antony Gardner   Artist: Susie Johns

Tissue Time!

TISSUE PAPER IS GREAT FOR MAKING COLLAGES. IT COMES IN A WIDE RANGE OF COLOURS AND IS SEMI-TRANSPARENT, SO YOU CAN GET SOME GREAT EFFECTS BY OVERLAPPING SHAPES.

YOU WILL NEED:

Large sheet of paper or card, coloured tissue paper, scissors, glue stick.

CUTE COUPLE

1) Cut shapes from coloured tissue. Try to cut them freehand, as pencil lines would spoil the effect of the finished picture.

2) Glue the shapes on to the background. Try to make sure some of the shapes overlap, as this looks very effective!

Top Tips!

Plan your picture by laying all the pieces down on your backing card before you glue.

Use small amounts of glue to keep it neat.

FLOWER POWER

INSTEAD OF CUTTING TISSUE, TRY TEARING IT INTO SHAPES.

A collage of a bunch of flowers, like this one, would make a great greetings card! I've even added a ribbon bow (by cutting two small slits in the paper and pushing the ends of the ribbon through) and a paper label!

Happy Birthday Mum !

TRY TO KEEP YOUR HANDS DRY AS THE COLOUR WILL RUN FROM THE TISSUE PAPER AND GET ON TO OTHER PAPER AND YOUR CLOTHES.

ART ATTACK

Colourful Circus!

PLAIN COLOURED PAPER, CUT INTO SHAPES, MAKES A REALLY COLOURFUL PICTURE. TAKE A LOOK HOW I MADE THESE AND THEN TRY IT YOURSELF!

1) Make the background by sticking large pieces of coloured paper to a sheet of card. You can overlap pieces to make the edges look neat.

2) Cut out figures such as a clown or a seal. If you are not confident about cutting these shapes freehand, you could trace them from this page on to the wrong side of your pieces of coloured paper. Stick the shapes in place, using a glue stick.

3) Cut out details from paper and stick these in place. Very fine details, such as eyes, can be added with a black marker pen.

YOU WILL NEED:

Large sheet of paper or card, coloured paper, scissors, glue stick.

TOP TIPS!

Save scraps of coloured paper wherever you can. You can often get coloured paper from old letters and envelopes. Magazines and catalogues are also a great source, the paper is often nice and shiny - and it won't cost you anything!

If you're not in the mood for straight lines, rip the paper rather than cut it. Tear it slowly and bit by bit to create the shapes you're after.

Sticky Souvenir!

NEXT TIME YOU GO ON HOLIDAY, OR FOR A DAY TRIP, SAVE ALL THE TICKETS, MAPS AND OTHER SCRAPS! THEN YOU CAN MAKE A COLLAGE TO REMIND YOU WHAT A GREAT TIME YOU HAD!

YOU WILL NEED:

large piece of paper or card,
coloured paper scraps (optional),
collection of tickets
and other souvenirs,
glue stick.

1) Arrange your bits and pieces on a piece of card until you are happy with the arrangement. You may need to trim some of the items, to fit, or stick them on to pieces of coloured paper, to make them stand out.

2) Stick down all the bits, using a glue stick. Overlap a few things as this will make it look busy and interesting.

3) Finally stick on labels which remind you where you have been.

favourite beach

AMGUEÐDFA WERIN CYMRU

TOCYN YMWELWR
Caniateir Mynediad am ddim

Llofnod
Dyddiad

My Girl Lisa
SWANSEA

CARDIFF

WHAT A GREAT KEEPSAKE! THIS IS ALSO A GREAT WAY TO SHOW YOUR TEACHER AND FRIENDS WHAT YOU DID IN THE HOLIDAYS.

ART ATTACK

← ancient monument

Entertainment Guide
Contact our Entertainments Team on
(01222) 239429 or 239412

Odeon Cinemas Limited VAT no. 425 2843 68

CIRCLE CINEMAS
SHOWING UNTIL THURSDAY
MAY change on Friday

ABC CARDIFF
INFO 01222 291715
BOOKING VISA · M'CARD
0541 555178

AUG FOR 7 DAYS

Odeon Cinemas Limited VAT no. 425 2843 68

ODEON
Sold subject to Odeon standard terms and conditions of purchase

Please retain this portion
Please retain this portion
55382150

CASTLE MUSEUM
CASTLE MUSEUM
CASTLE MUSEUM
CASTLE MUSEUM
'S TOWER "
NCESSION
3522

CARDIFF

ODEON ROW SEAT   12.8   DAT

DWEEZEL'S PLAY CENTRE
ASDA SUPERSTORE
FERRY ROAD
CARDIFF BAY

← on the ferry

carnival →

holiday cottage →

CG   997307
410

Adult
Child

TECHNIQUEST

MAIN EXHIBITION
Please Retain This Ticket

Stryd Stuart Caerdydd CF1 6BW   01222 475 475   Stuart Street Cardiff CF1 6BW

When taking photos, take an extra couple
to stick on your souvenir collage.

If all the collage pieces are rectangular or square - like tickets, photos and maps -
make some of the things circular. (Just draw round a glass and cut it out.)

Fame Frames!

FRAME A POP STAR PIN-UP
OR MOVIE IDOL, OR A
FAVOURITE PHOTOGRAPH,
WITH CUT-OUTS FROM
MAGAZINES OR COMICS.

YOU WILL NEED:

Cardboard box card,
collection of old magazines
and comics, coloured paper
scraps (optional),
glue stick.

1. Cut a frame shape from cardboard box card.

2. Cut out pictures from magazines of all your favourite movie and pop stars.

3. Stick the cut-outs all over the frame, using a glue stick, until the cardboard is completely covered.

Top Tips!

You can secure it to the wall with sticky tack or, alternatively, you can make a stand to go on the back using a rectangle of card and sticky tape.

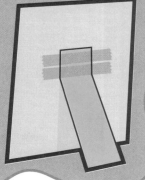

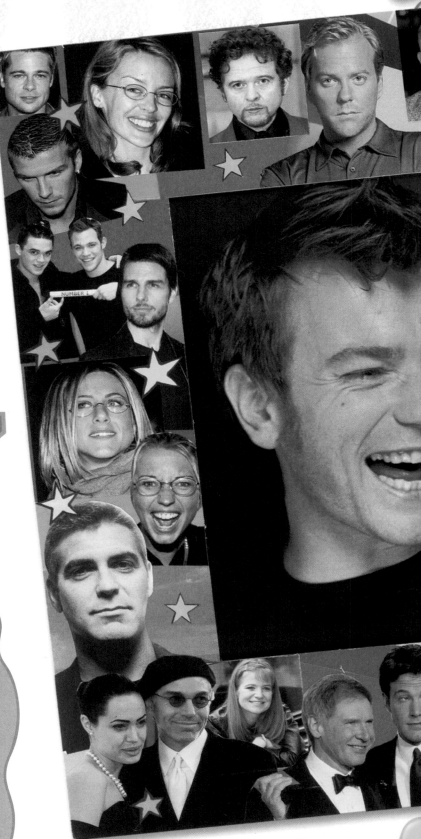

Shine On!

SAVE SHINY SWEET WRAPPERS AND COMBINE THEM WITH PLAIN COLOURED PAPER TO MAKE A REGAL PORTRAIT.

YOU WILL NEED:

coloured foil sweet wrappers,
black card,
scraps of coloured paper,
metallic paper,
glue stick,
fake jewels,
PVA glue.

1) Cut out shapes for the face and neck from coloured paper. You can draw the shapes first, on the wrong side of the paper (so the pencil lines won't show when you cut them out), or just cut them out freehand. Stick the pieces on a large sheet of black paper.

2) Make a crown from gold foil. First crumple the foil, then smooth it out again and stick it, using a glue stick, to a scrap of card. Then cut out the crown shape and stick it in place.

3) Cut out other shapes, like stars, from coloured or metallic card and stick in place. For buttons or jewels, try crumpling foil into balls, or use foil to cover small discs of card, before sticking in place.

4) Add a bit of extra opulence by sticking on a few fake jewels, using PVA glue.

All That Glitters!

MAGICAL MERMAID

Use sparkly and holographic papers. Look out for shiny wrapping paper or self-adhesive book-covering film, available at stationers and craft shops.

1) Stick the A4 sheet of blue paper in the centre of the larger piece of paper or card. Cut 2 cm squares of coloured and sparkly papers and stick these around the edge of the blue paper to make a patchwork border.

2) Cut out the mermaid's head and body, two small circles for cheeks and a rock for her to sit on, from coloured paper. Stick these in place. The body and arms can be in one piece. Cut out eight tiny sausage shapes, too, for fingers, and keep these to one side for now. Cut out eyes and the mouth from black paper (or draw them, using a black pen).

3) Cut the tail, hair, mirror and comb from shiny and sparkly papers, and stick these in place. Now you can carefully stick the fingers on top of the mirror and comb handles.

4) From scraps of sparkly and shiny papers, cut seaweed and fish. Cut out an oval shape, for the mirror glass, from silver card.

HOW ABOUT ADDING SOME SPARKLE AND GLITZ TO YOU COLLAGE CREATIONS. DARE TO DAZZLE WITH THESE SIMPLE IDEAS!

YOU WILL NEED:

sheet of A3 paper or card,
sheet of blue A4 paper,
sparkly paper,
scrap of shiny silver card,
coloured paper scraps,
glue stick,
glitter,
sequins.

SUPER SEAHORSE

This picture is made in the same way as the mermaid. Stick on sequins for extra sparkle, and outline shapes with glitter or glitter glue.

Top Tips!

If you are using loose glitter, cover the work surface with newspaper first. This way you can shake the excess on to the paper and pour back into the container.

If you haven't got any metallic or sparkly paper, shiny sweet wrappers and silver foil can be used.

In The Picture!

THIS IS TWO PICTURES IN ONE!

MAKE A MONTAGE FROM PHOTOS OF YOUR FAMILY AND FRIENDS AND A BACKGROUND FROM COLOURED PAPER SHAPES!

If you are not allowed to cut up actual photographs, get photocopies made and cut these.

YOU WILL NEED:

photographs (or photocopies),
large sheet of coloured paper or card,
scraps of coloured paper,
glue stick.

1) On a large sheet of coloured paper (I used pale blue), stick house shapes in different colours or shades of one colour, such as grey or beige. The house shapes are just tall rectangles with a roof shape cut out of one end of each.

2) Cut thin strips and small rectangles of black paper and stick on to make windows, windowsills and doors.

3) Cut out individual people from your photos or photocopies and arrange them, overlapping, at the bottom of your picture. When you are satisfied with the arrangement, stick them in place with glue.

4) As a finishing touch, you could add cut-out white paper clouds and a yellow circle for the sun.

HALLOWE'EN HELLO!

WHAT ABOUT USING THIS IDEA TO CREATE GREETINGS CARDS OR UNIQUE PARTY INVITES? HERE'S AN IDEA FOR HALLOWE'EN.

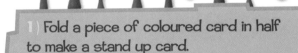

HAPPY HALLOWEEN

1) Fold a piece of coloured card in half to make a stand up card.

2) Cut out a photo of yourself or a friend and stick it on the front.

3) Use coloured card to decorate it – I used black paper to transform it into a Hallowe'en card.

GET YOUR FRIENDS TO EACH GIVE YOU A PICTURE AND CREATE A PHOTO MONTAGE OF YOUR CLASS. GO ON TRY IT YOURSELF!

Top Of The Crop

GRAIN

YOU WILL NEED:

Large piece of card for background (cardboard box card is ideal), corrugated paper, glue stick, PVA glue, wooden lolly sticks, scraps of fabric, raffia, 2 buttons, 2 goggly eyes, melon seeds.

CREATE TEXTURE IN YOUR PICTURES USING CORRUGATED PAPER OR CARD. SEE HOW THE RIDGES LOOK A BIT LIKE PLOUGHED FIELDS IN THIS PICTURE.

1) Make the background. Cover the top part of the cardboard with blue paper, for the sky. Cut out fields, hills and trees from corrugated paper - brown, yellow, green and white. Stick them down using a glue stick.

2) Cut out the scarecrow's coat from fabric. Or you could use paper. Cut out a head, too, and a hat. Glue lolly sticks in place, one vertical and one horizontal, using PVA, then glue the other bits of the scarecrow in place, including some bits of raffia for his hair and in his sleeves.

3) Now add all the other details - cut a sack shape from fabric and glue on seeds (these are melon seeds, washed and dried), black paper crows with goggly eyes, trees and a broken fence made from painted lolly sticks.

Top Tips!

You can buy coloured corrugated paper from craft shops. or save corrugated packaging from boxes and paint it different colours, using poster paints or acrylics, before cutting out your shapes.

A glue stick is ideal for sticking paper, including corrugated paper. For fabric, cover with a thin layer of PVA. PVA is also ideal for sticking small objects such as buttons, seeds and lolly sticks.

Feelin' Gifted!

DAZZLE WITH DECOUPAGE - MAKE GREETINGS CARDS AND GIFT BOXES USING THIS EASY AND FUN METHOD OF DECORATING SURFACES WITH PAPER CUT-OUTS!

GREETINGS CARDS

1) Fold coloured or white card in half to make your card. It needs to be thick enough to stand up but it can be any shape - square, rectangular, narrow or wide...

2) Stick a smaller square of different coloured card on the front to make the card more three dimensional.

3) Now cut out pictures and paste them onto the front using paper glue - I used butterflies and flowers to decorate my cards.

GIFT BOX

1) How about making a gift box to match your card? You can use a box you already have or make one from thick pieces of card. Stick the bits together and cover with 2 layers of torn newspaper pasted on with PVA glue.

2) Paint the whole box inside and out and leave to dry.

3) As with the card, paste pictures onto the box using PVA glue. Leave to dry.

YOU WILL NEED:

coloured card,
paper glue,
newspaper,
gift wrapping or pictures,

PVA glue,
thick card,
sticky tape,
paints.

TOP TIPS!

Use gift wrapping to get lots of images of the same picture - like these butterflies and flowers. Having the same images on a card and gift box look brilliant!

ART ATTACK

Bug Out

FOR AN ULTRA-3D EFFECT, CUT SHAPES FROM THICK CARD AND COVER EACH ONE WITH PAPER!

LOOK AT THESE FUNNY, SCARY BUGS! COPY THESE OR MAKE UP YOUR OWN WITH WILD COMBINATIONS OF COLOURS AND THE FUNNIEST FACES!

1) For a body, cut a circle of card and cover it with paper. Add stripes or spots - or both - by sticking on bits of paper in a contrasting colour. Cut a smaller circle or other shape for a head.

2) Stick lengths of pipe cleaners to the back of the bug, for legs and antennae. You can push beads on to the ends of the pipe cleaners, if you like!

3) Glue on goggly eyes, using PVA glue. Stick the bugs to backing card.

Top Tips!

To make the bodies, how about using plastic lids? Use double-sided sticky tape or glue to cover them with coloured paper.

You can decorate your bugs with colourful stickers or you could paint them.

YOU WILL NEED:
scraps of thick card,
piece of card for background,
coloured paper,
pipe cleaners,
beads,
glue stick,
PVA glue.

WHAT ABOUT BUGGING SOMEONE ELSE!

Secure some thread to the back of your bug and hang up - in the fridge, in the car, in a cupboard, in the bathroom cabinet - anywhere you can bug someone!

Sail Away!

THIS TIME, RATHER THAN USING COLOURED PAPER, PAINT WHITE PAPER IN YOUR OWN CHOICE OF COLOURS AND CREATE THIS COLOURFUL YACHT RACE!

Not only does this method mean you can choose your own colours and patterns, but the painted pieces have an attractive texture. Try it yourself!

1) Firstly, paint a large sheet of paper turquoise blue, for the sea. Paint another wide strip of paper sky blue.

2) Paint scraps of paper with plain colours or with spots and stripes. Leave to dry.

3) With a black marker pen, draw sails, flags and hulls on top of the painted pieces of paper. Cut out around these black lines. Make a lighthouse and some clouds in the same way.

4) Stick the sea and sky on to the background. Stick the boats, lighthouse and clouds in place using just a dab of glue on the back of each piece, so they stick up slightly from the background, creating a slightly 3D effect.

5) Stick a cut-to-size straw in between the sails to make a mast.

Top Tips!

Use thicker paper or thin card to draw your boats on - this will make them really stand out from the background.

24

YOU WILL NEED:

Thick paper,
PVA glue,
acrylic paints or poster paints,
black marker pen,
large sheet of card for background,
paper drinking straws.

A SINGLE BOAT LOOKS VERY EFFECTIVE.
HERE I'VE USED A LOLLIPOP STICK AS A SAIL
AND BLUE CORRUGATED PAPER FOR THE SEA!

HiNTS AND TiPS!

A lot of the materials used in collage you will probably already have or at least be able to get hold of very easily! Save scraps of paper and card – as many different kinds as you can – to give as much colour and texture as possible to your projects.

HERE ARE A FEW THINGS YOU CAN COLLECT:

coloured paper
envelopes
magazines
comics
cardboard box card
sweet wrappers
lolly sticks
wrapping paper
string

HERE ARE A FEW THINGS YOU MAY HAVE TO BUY:

glue stick
PVA glue
glitter glue
sticky tape
pipe cleaners
goggly eyes
corrugated paper
sequins

THIS PICTURE OF A ROCKET SHOWS HOW YOU CAN ACHIEVE TEXTURED EFFECTS QUITE SIMPLY.

The body of the rocket is cut from some fancy silver corrugated card and the fins from shiny silver card. The nose cone and booster are coloured foil from chocolates. The big gold star is cut from gold corrugated card and the other stars are the gummed ones you can buy in packets from stationers. The lettering is cut from sparkly self-adhesive book covering paper.

rocket